For

Words of Love

Compiled by
Sophia Bedford-Pierce

Design by
Evelyn Beilenson
and
Solomon M. Skolnick

PETER PAUPER PRESS, INC.
WHITE PLAINS · NEW YORK

Copyright © 1995
Peter Pauper Press, Inc.
202 Mamaroneck Avenue
White Plains, NY 10601
All rights reserved
ISBN 0-88088-590-4
Printed in Hong Kong
7 6 5 4 3 2 1

Table of Contents

Words of Love

Take away love, and our earth is a tomb.

ROBERT BROWNING

Know you the land where the lemon-trees bloom? In the dark foliage the gold oranges glow, a soft wind hovers from the sky, the myrtle is still and the laurel stands tall—do you know it well? There, there, I would go, O my beloved, with thee!

JOHANN WOLFGANG VON GOETHE

Sonnet

Shall I compare thee to a Summer's day?
Thou art more lovely and more temperate:
Rough winds do shake the darling buds of May,
And Summer's lease hath all too short a date:
Sometime too hot the eye of heaven shines,
And often is his gold complexion dimm'd;
And every fair from fair sometime declines,
By chance, or nature's changing course
 untrimm'd:
But thy eternal Summer shall not fade
Nor loose possession of that fair thou ow'st;
Nor shall Death brag thou wand'rest in his shade,
When in eternal lines to time thou grow'st:
So long as men can breathe or eyes can see,
So long lives this and this gives life to thee.

WILLIAM SHAKESPEARE

You'll Love Me Yet!

You'll love me yet! And I can tarry
Your love's protracted growing.
June reared that bunch of flowers you carry
From seeds of April's sowing.

I plant a heartful now; some seed
At least is sure to strike
And yield—what you'll not pluck indeed,
Not love, but, may be, like.

You'll look at least on love's remains,
A grave's one violet.
Your look?—that pays a thousand pains—
What's death! You'll love me yet!

ROBERT BROWNING

How Do I Love Thee?

How do I love thee? Let me count the ways
I love thee to the depth and breadth and height
My soul can reach, when feeling out of sight
For the ends of Being and ideal Grace.
I love thee to the level of everyday's
Most quiet need, by sun and candle-light.
I love thee freely, as men strive for Right;
I love thee purely, as they turn from Praise.
I love thee with the passion put to use
In my old griefs, and with my childhood's faith.
I love thee with a love I seemed to lose
With my lost saints,— I love thee with
   the breath,
Smiles, tears, of all my life!—and, if God choose,
I shall but love thee better after death.

ELIZABETH BARRETT BROWNING

7

Unable are the Loved to die
For Love is Immortality.

EMILY DICKINSON

I Had A Garden

I had a garden where for sunless days
And many starless nights the dusky ways
Were weed-o'ergrown and silent. There I heard
No voice of love low calling to its own,
And found nor joy nor beauty; but alone
I lived, till through the silence, like a bird
Full-throated, came the music of a friend.

LOUIS V. LEDOUX

My Heart Is Like A Singing Bird

My heart is like a singing bird
   Whose nest is in a water'd shoot;
My heart is like an apple-tree
   Whose boughs are bent with thick-set fruit;
My heart is like a rainbow shell
   That paddles in a halcyon sea;
My heart is gladder than all these
   Because my true love is come to me.

CHRISTINA ROSSETTI

Such Is True Love

Such is true love, which steals into the heart
With feet as silent as the lightsome dawn
That kisses smooth the rough brown of the dark,
And hath its will through blissful gentleness,
Not like a rocket, which, with passionate glare,
Whirs suddenly up, then bursts, and leaves the
    night
Painfully quivering on the dazèd eyes;
A love that gives and takes, that seeth faults,
Not with flaw-seeking eyes like needle points,
But loving-kindly ever looks them down
With the o'ercoming faith that still forgives;
A love that shall be new and fresh each hour,
As is the sunset's golden mystery
Or the sweet coming of the evening-star,
Alike, and yet most unlike, every day,
And seeming ever best and fairest now.

JAMES RUSSELL LOWELL

11

Love

I love you,
Not only for what you are,
But for what I am
When I am with you.

I love you,
Not only for what
You have made of yourself,
But for what
You are making of me.

I love you
For the part of me
That you bring out;
I love you
For putting your hand
Into my heaped-up heart
And passing over
All the foolish, weak things
That you can't help
Dimly seeing there,
And for drawing out
Into the light
All the beautiful belongings
That no one else had looked
Quite far enough to find.

I love you because you
Are helping me to make

Of the lumber of my life
Not a tavern,
But a temple;
Out of the works
Of my every day
Not a reproach
But a song.

I love you
Because you have done
More than any creed
Could have done
To make me good,
And more than any fate
Could have done
To make me happy.

You have done it
Without a touch,
Without a word,
Without a sign.
You have done it
By being yourself.
Perhaps that is what
Being a friend means,
After all.

ROY CROFT

Who ever loved, that loved not at first sight?

CHRISTOPHER MARLOWE

Love reckons hours for months, and days for years; and every little absence is an age.

JOHN DRYDEN

And what is a kiss, when all is done?
A promise given under seal!—a vow
A signature acknowledged—a rosy dot
Over the i of Loving—a secret whispered
To listening lips apart—a moment made
Immortal, with a rush of wings unseen—
A sacrament of blossoms, a new song
Sung by two hearts to an old simple tune—
The ring of one horizon around two souls
Together, all alone!

EDMOND ROSTAND

You bound strong sandals on my feet,
  You gave me bread and wine,
And sent me under sun and stars,
  For all the world was mine.

Oh take the sandals off my feet,
  You know not what to do;
For all my world is in your arms,
  My sun and stars are you.

SARA TEASDALE

I think true love is never blind,
  But rather brings an added light,
An inner vision quick to find
  The beauties hid from common sight.

No soul can ever clearly see
  Another's highest, noblest part,
Save through the sweet philosophy
  And loving wisdom of the heart.

PHOEBE CARY

If Thou Must Love Me

If thou must love me, let it be for naught
Except for love's sake only. Do not say:
"I love her for her smile, . . . her look, . . .
   her way
Of speaking gently, . . . for a trick of thought
That falls in well with mine, and certes brought
A sense of pleasant ease on such a day"—
For these things in themselves, Belovèd, may
Be changed or change for thee,— and love
   so wrought
May be unwrought so. Neither love me for
Thine own dear pity's wiping my cheeks dry:
A creature might well forget to weep who bore
Thy comfort long, and lose thy love thereby.
But love me for love's sake, that evermore
Thou may'st love on through love's eternity.

ELIZABETH BARRETT BROWNING

17

The Indian Serenade

I arise from dreams of thee
In the first sweet sleep of night,
When the winds are breathing low,
And the stars are shining bright:
I arise from dreams of thee,
And a spirit in my feet
Hath led me—who knows how?
To thy chamber window, Sweet!

The wandering airs they faint
On the dark, the silent stream—
And the Champak's odors fail
Like sweet thoughts in a dream;
The nightingale's complaint,
It dies upon her heart;—
As I must on thine,
O! belovèd as thou art!

O lift me from the grass!
I die! I faint! I fail!
Let thy love in kisses rain
On my lips and eyelids pale.
My cheek is cold and white, alas!
My heart beats loud and fast;—
Oh! press it close to thine again,
Where it will break at last.

PERCY BYSSHE SHELLEY

It is difficult to know at what moment love begins; it is less difficult to know it has begun.

HENRY WADSWORTH LONGFELLOW

Love doesn't grow on trees like apples in Eden —it's something that you have to make. And you must use your imagination too. . . .

JOYCE CARY

If Love Be Love

In Love, if Love be Love; if Love be ours,
Faith and unfaith can ne'er be equal powers:
Unfaith in aught is want of faith in all.

It is the little rift within the lute,
That by and by will make the music mute,
And ever widening slowly silence all.

The little rift within the lover's lute
Or little pitted speck in garner'd fruit,
That rotting inward slowly moulders all.

It is not worth the keeping: let it go:
But shall it? answer, darling, answer, no
And trust me not at all or all in all.

ALFRED, LORD TENNYSON

21

Parting

My life closed twice before its close;
It yet remains to see
If Immortality unveil
A third event to me.

So huge, so hopeless to conceive
As these that twice befell.
Parting is all we know of heaven
And all we need of hell.

EMILY DICKINSON

Doubt that the stars are fire;
Doubt that the sun doth move;
Doubt truth to be a liar;
But never doubt I love.

WILLIAM SHAKESPEARE,
Hamlet

22

Alas, that Spring should vanish with the Rose!
That Youth's sweet-scented manuscript should
  close!
The Nightingale that in the branches sang,
Ah, whence, and whither flown again, who
  knows!

Ah Love! could thou and I with Fate conspire
To grasp this sorry Scheme of Things entire,
Would not we shatter it to bits and then
Re-mould it nearer to the Heart's Desire?

EDWARD FITZGERALD,
Rubaiyat of Omar Khayyam

We are shaped and fashioned by what we love.

JOHANN WOLFGANG VON GOETHE

Set me as a seal upon thine heart;
As a seal upon thine arm:
For love is strong as death;
Jealousy is cruel as the grave,
The flashes thereof are flashes of fire,
A very flame of the Lord.
Many waters cannot quench love,
Neither can the floods drown it. . . .

KING SOLOMON

Sonnet

Let me not to the marriage of true minds
Admit impediments. Love is not love
Which alters when it alteration finds,
Or bends with the remover to remove:
O, no! it is an ever-fixèd mark,
That looks on tempests and is never shaken;
It is the star to every wand'ring bark,
Whose worth's unknown, although his height
  be taken.
Love's not Time's fool, though rosy lips and cheeks
Within his bending sickle's compass come;
Love alters not with his brief hours and weeks,
But bears it out even to the edge of doom,—
If this be error and upon me provèd,
I never writ, nor no man ever lovèd.

WILLIAM SHAKESPEARE

Wild nights! Wild nights!
Were I with thee,
Wild nights should be
Our luxury!

Futile the winds
To a heart in port,
Done with the compass,
Done with the chart.

Rowing in Eden!
Ah! the sea!
Might I but moor
To-night in thee!

EMILY DICKINSON

Believe Me If All Those Endearing Young Charms

Believe me, if all those endearing young charms
Which I gaze on so fondly today
Were to fade by tomorrow and fleet in my arms
Like fairy gifts fading away,
Thou wouldst still be adored as this moment
    thou art,
Let thy loveliness fade as it will,
And around the dear ruin each wish of my heart
Would entwine itself verdantly still.

It is not while beauty and youth are thine own
And thy cheeks unprofaned by a tear
That the fervor and faith of a soul can be known
To which time will but make thee more dear.
No, the heart that has truly loved never forgets
But as truly loves on to the close—
As the sunflower turns on her god when he sets
The same look which she turned when he rose.

THOMAS MOORE

27

You know that when I hate you, it is because I love you to a point of passion that unhinges my soul.

JULIE-JEANNE-ELÉONORE DE LESPINASSE

Love is a mighty god, you know,
   That rules with potent sway;
And when he draws his awful bow,
   We mortals must obey.

MARY MASTERS

Echo

Come to me in the silence of the night;
Come in the speaking silence of a dream;
Come with soft rounded cheeks and eyes as
   bright
As sunlight on a stream;
Come back in tears,
O memory, hope, love of finished years.

O dream how sweet, too sweet, too bitter-sweet,
Whose wakening should have been in Paradise,
Where souls brim-full of love abide and meet;
Where thirsty longing eyes
Watch the slow door
That opening, letting in, lets out no more.

Yet come to me in dreams, that I may live
My very life again though cold in death;
Come back to me in dreams, that I may give
Pulse for pulse, breath for breath:
Speak low, lean low,
As long ago my love, how long ago.

CHRISTINA ROSSETTI

Love is a circle that doth restless move
In the same sweet eternity of love.

ROBERT HERRICK

She Walks In Beauty

She walks in beauty, like the night
    Of cloudless climes and starry skies,
And all that's best of dark and bright
    Meets in her aspect and her eyes,
Thus mellowed to that tender light
    Which heaven to gaudy day denies.

One shade the more, one ray the less
    Had half impaired the nameless grace
Which waves in every raven tress
    Or softly lightens o'er her face,
Where thoughts serenely sweet express
    How pure, how dear their dwelling-place.

And on that cheek and o'er that brow
    So soft, so calm, yet eloquent,
The smiles that win, the tints that glow,
    But tell of days in goodness spent,—
A mind at peace with all below,
    A heart whose love is innocent.

LORD BYRON

Give All To Love

Give all to love;
Obey thy heart;
Friends, kindred, days,
Estate, good-fame,
Plans, credit, and the Muse,—
Nothing refuse.

'Tis a brave master;
Let it have scope:
Follow it utterly,
Hope beyond hope:
High and more high
It dives into noon,
With wing unspent,
Untold intent;
But it is a god,
Knows its own path,
And the outlets of the sky.

It was not for the mean;
It requireth courage stout,
Souls above doubt,
Valor unbending;
It will reward,—
They shall return
More than they were,
And ever ascending.

Leave all for love;
Yet, hear me, yet,

One word more thy heart behoved,
One pulse more of firm endeavor,—
Keep thee today,
To-morrow forever,
Free as an Arab
Of thy beloved.

Cling with life to the maid;
But when the surprise,
First vague shadow of surmise
Flits across her bosom young
Of a joy apart from thee,
Free be she, fancy-free;
Nor thou detain her vesture's hem,
Nor the palest rose she flung
From her summer diadem.

RALPH WALDO EMERSON

The Blackbird

The nightingale has a lyre of gold,
  The lark's is a clarion call,
And the blackbird plays but a boxwood flute,
  But I love him best of all.

For his song is all of the joy of life,
  And we in the mad, spring weather,
We two have listened till he sang
  Our hearts and lips together.

WILLIAM E. HENLEY

June

Last June I saw your face three times,
   Three times I touched your hand;
Now, as before, May month is o'er,
   And June is in the land.

O many Junes shall come and go,
   Flower-footed o'er the mead;
O many Junes for me, to whom
   Is length of days decreed.

There shall be sunlight, scent of rose,
   Warm mist of Summer rain;
Only this change—I shall not look
   Upon your face again.

AMY LEVY

Sonnet

Who will believe my verse in time to come,
If it were fill'd with your most high deserts?
Though yet, heaven knows, it is but as a tomb
Which hides your life and shows not half your
    parts.
If I could write the beauty of your eyes
And in fresh numbers number all your graces,
The age to come would say "This Poet lies;
Such heavenly touches ne'er touch'd earthly
    faces."
So should my papers, yellow'd with their age,
Be scorn'd like old men of less truth than tongue,
And your true rights be termed a Poet's rage:
And stretchèd metre of an antique song:
But were some child of yours alive that time,
You should live twice; in it and in my rhyme.

WILLIAM SHAKESPEARE

36

Love sought is good, but given unsought, is
better.

WILLIAM SHAKESPEARE,
Twelfth Night

How silver-sweet sound lovers' tongues by
night, like softest music to attending ears.

WILLIAM SHAKESPEARE,
Romeo and Juliet

Absence

Music, when soft voices die,
Vibrates in the memory;
Odors, when sweet violets sicken,
Live within the sense they quicken.

Rose leaves, when the rose is dead,
Are heap'd for the belovèd's bed;
And so thy thoughts, when thou art gone,
Love itself shall slumber on.

PERCY BYSSHE SHELLEY

When I Think

Belovèd, my Belovèd, when I think
That thou wast in the world a year ago,
What time I sat alone here in the snow
And saw no footprint, heard the silence sink
No moment at thy voice, . . . but, link by link,
When counting all my chains, as if that so
They never could fall off at any blow
Struck by thy possible hand . . . why, thus
   I drink
Of life's great cup of wonder! Wonderful
Never to feel thee thrill the day or night
With personal act or speech—nor ever cull
Some prescience of thee with the blossoms white
Thou sawest growing! Atheists are as dull
Who cannot guess God's presence out of sight.

ELIZABETH BARRETT BROWNING

Bedouin Song

From the desert I come to thee
On a stallion shod with fire;
And the winds are left behind
In the speed of my desire.
Under thy window I stand
And the midnight hears my cry:
I love thee, I love but thee,
With a love that cannot die
Till the sun grows cold,
And the stars are old,
And the leaves of the Judgment Book unfold!

Look from thy window and see
My passion and my pain;
I lie on the sands below
And I faint in thy disdain.
Let the night-winds touch thy brow
With the heat of my burning sigh,
And melt thee to hear the vow
Of a love that shall not die
Till the sun grows cold
And the stars are old
And the leaves of the Judgment Book unfold!

My steps are nightly driven
By the fever in my breast
To hear from thy lattice breathed
The word that shall give me rest.
Open the door of thy heart

And open thy chamber door,
And my kisses shall teach thy lips
The love that shall fade no more
Till the sun grows cold
And the stars are old
And the leaves of the Judgment Book unfold!

BAYARD TAYLOR

Love Not Me
For Comely Grace

Love not me for comely grace,
For my pleasing eye or face,
Nor for any outward part,
No, nor for my constant heart;
   For those may fail or turn to ill,
     So thou and I shall sever;
Keep therefore a true woman's eye,
And love me still, but know not why.
   So hast thou the same reason still
     To dote upon me ever.

ANONYMOUS

Remember my unalterable maxim,—When we love, we have always something to say.

LADY MARY WORTLEY MONTAGUE

Let him kiss me with the kisses of his mouth: for thy love is better than wine.

KING SOLOMON

Song

Nay! if thou must depart, thou shalt depart;
But why so soon—oh, heart-blood of my heart?
Go then! yet — going — turn and stay thy feet,
That I may once more see that face so sweet.
Once more — if never more; for swift days go
As hastening waters from their fountains flow;
And whether yet again shall meeting be
Who knows? Who knows? Ah! turn once more
to me.

EDWIN ARNOLD

And first an hour of mournful musing,
And then a gush of bitter tears,
And then a dreary calm diffusing
Its deadly mist o'er joys and cares;
And then a throb, and then a lightening,
And then a breathing from above,
And then a star in heaven brightening —
The start, the glorious star of love.

EMILY BRONTË

Ah! What Is Love?

Ah! What is love? It is a pretty thing,
As sweet unto a shepherd as a king,
      And sweeter too;
For kings have cares that wait upon a crown,
And cares can make the sweetest face
  to frown:
      Ah then, ah then,
If country loves such sweet desires gain,
What lady would not love a shepherd swain?

His flocks are folded; he comes home at night
As merry as a king in his delight,
      And merrier too;
For kings bethink them what the state require,
Where shepherds, careless, carol by the fire:
      Ah then, ah then,
If country loves such sweet desires gain,
What lady would not love a shepherd swain?

He kisseth first, then sits as blithe to eat
His cream and curd as doth the king his meat,
      And blither too;
For kings have often fears when they sup,
Where shepherds dread no poison in their cup:

        Ah then, ah then,
If country loves such sweet desires gain,
What lady would not love a shepherd swain?

Upon his couch of straw he sleeps as sound
As doth the king upon his beds of down,
        More sounder too;
For cares cause kings full oft their sleep to spill,
Where weary shepherds lie and snort their fill:
        Ah then, ah then,
If country loves such sweet desires gain,
What lady would not love a shepherd swain?

Thus with his wife he spends the year as blithe
As doth the king at every tide or syth,
        And blither too;
For kings have wars and broils to take in hand,
When shepherds laugh, and love upon the land:
        Ah then, ah then,
If country loves such sweet desires gain,
What lady would not love a shepherd swain?

ROBERT GREENE

47

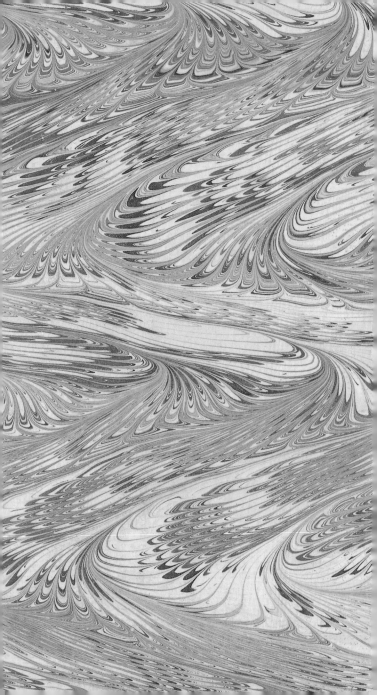